D1709223

INSIDE THE
GOLD
INDUSTRY

by M. M. Eboch

Content Consultant

Andrea Brickey, PhD

Associate Professor—Mining Engineering
and Management
South Dakota School of Mines & Technology

Essential Library

An Imprint of Abdo Publishing | abdopublishing.com

abdopublishing.com

Published by Abdo Publishing, a division of ABDO, PO Box 398166, Minneapolis, Minnesota 55439. Copyright © 2017 by Abdo Consulting Group, Inc. International copyrights reserved in all countries. No part of this book may be reproduced in any form without written permission from the publisher. Essential Library™ is a trademark and logo of Abdo Publishing.

Printed in the United States of America, North Mankato, Minnesota
092016
012017

THIS BOOK CONTAINS
RECYCLED MATERIALS

Cover Photo: Sarin Kunthong/Shutterstock Images
Interior Photos: Sarin Kunthong/Shutterstock Images, 1; NASA/JPL-Caltech, 4; NASA, 9; Kenneth Garrett/Danita Delimont Photography/Newscom, 10; North Wind Picture Archives, 15, 25, 26, 28, 30, 32; Repina Valeriya/Shutterstock Images, 18; Jeffrey B. Banke/Shutterstock Images, 20; Gilles Paire/iStockphoto, 22; NASA/GSFC/METI/ERSDAC/JAROS, and U.S./Japan ASTER Science Team, 35; Vuk Markovic/AP Images, 37; Shutterstock Images, 40, 50, 54; TT Studio/Shutterstock Images, 42–43; Graeme Williams/South Photographs/africanpictures.net/Newscom, 44; Steve Lovegrove/Shutterstock Images, 46; Red Line Editorial, 48, 96–97; Johan Ordonez/AFP/Getty Images, 52; Carla Gottgens/Bloomberg/Getty Images, 56; Rodrigo Abd/AP Images, 58, 70; Westend61/Florian Kopp/Newscom, 60–61; Joao Luiz Bulcao/Polaris/Newscom, 66; Dean Hutton/Bloomberg/Getty Images, 74–75; Brennan Linsley/AP Images, 76; G. A. Rossi/Picture-Alliance/DPA/AP Images, 78–79; Joerg Boethling/Alamy Stock Photo, 82; Ingram Publishing/Newscom, 86; Benny Sieu/Milwaukee Journal Sentinel/MCT/Newscom, 90–91; Michael S. Lewis/Getty Images, 94

Editor: Mirella Miller
Series Designer: Craig Hinton

Publisher's Cataloging-in-Publication Data

Names: Eboch, M. M., author.
Title: Inside the gold industry / by M. M. Eboch.
Description: Minneapolis, MN : Abdo Publishing, 2017. | Series: Big business | Includes bibliographical references and index.
Identifiers: LCCN 2016945199 | ISBN 9781680783711 (lib. bdg.) | ISBN 9781680797244 (ebook)
Subjects: LCSH: Gold industry--Juvenile literature. | Gold products--Juvenile literature.
Classification: DDC 338--dc23
LC record available at http://lccn.loc.gov/2016945199

Contents

1 GOLD IN SPACE

The Mars Global Surveyor, which functioned from 1996 to 2006, mapped Mars using a gold-plated telescope mirror. The purpose of using gold on the telescope was not to show off or to waste money. Rather, the US National Aeronautics and Space Administration (NASA) uses gold for its reflective ability. The Mars Global Surveyor used the telescope to chart the surface features of Mars. The gold plating on the mirror captured infrared radiation that had bounced back from the planet's surface.

Gold has special properties that make it ideal for a variety of unusual purposes. It is one of the best materials for reflecting infrared radiation, a type of invisible energy that is felt as heat. Gold can also be applied in an extremely thin coating. Many parts of space vehicles use a thin gold film. By reflecting the infrared radiation, the film helps control the temperature inside the spacecraft. A thin layer of gold is also used on astronaut helmets to filter out the sun's dangerous rays. Closer to Earth, many satellites are protected from solar heat by gold-coated films. And this is only one of the unusual uses of gold, in space and on our planet.

Without gold, the Mars Global Surveyor could not have done its job.

HIDDEN GOLD

Gold has been valued for thousands of years, as money and to make precious objects, especially jewelry. For jewelry, gold is valued for its shiny, rich color and the tradition that claims gold is valuable. Gold's properties as a metal are also beneficial in jewelry making. It is easily worked and can be hammered into thin sheets, drawn into narrow wires, or cast into a variety of shapes. In addition, gold does not tarnish easily, so it remains shiny and bright for a long time. Many other metals are harder to work, tarnish quickly, or are dull with plain colors.

Golden Mirrors

Space telescopes often use microscopically thin layers of gold. NASA's James Webb Space Telescope has 18 mirror segments that each received gold coatings approximately one-millionth of an inch thick. These coatings are 200 times thinner than a human hair, and yet the gold remains durable and reflective.[1] This provides a light-gathering ability that helps scientists study the most distant objects in the universe. The James Webb Space Telescope is scheduled to launch in 2018.

Gold's physical qualities are also ideal for many electronic uses. Gold is so easy to work that it can be drawn into a wire a fraction of the thickness of a human hair. It can be beaten into a sheet so thin it is translucent. Therefore, gold can be used for very fine, even microscopic, electronic parts.

Resistance to tarnish is extremely important for any metal used in electronics. Many electronic devices use very low voltages and currents. The flow of electricity can be easily interrupted if there is any corrosion or tarnish in the system. Electronic components made with gold are highly reliable, as they rarely corrode.

Many electronic devices, from cell phones to television sets, contain small amounts of gold. Mobile phones contain an average of 33 gold-plated contact points, a type of switch to turn the electric current on or off. This averages 0.001 ounces (0.034 g) of gold per phone, which is worth less than two dollars.[2] Computers also use gold in many electronic parts. The reliability and high conductivity of gold is ideal for quickly and accurately transmitting digital data between components.

GOLD'S VALUE IN SPACE

For these same reasons, gold is used in space vehicle electronics. In fact, NASA uses gold throughout its spacecraft. Space travel can cost billions of dollars, and once a vehicle is launched it is difficult or impossible to repair. Therefore, the most reliable materials must be used. Because gold does not corrode, any electronics found in spacecraft are likely to have gold components.

Spacecraft also use very thin films of gold between some moving parts. Two sheets of gold will slide past each other easily, so the gold acts as a

Mixing Metals

Pure gold is too soft to stand up to rough use. A ring made of pure gold would quickly be damaged through normal wear. Therefore, gold is often alloyed, or combined, with other metals, such as silver, copper, or platinum. Mixing gold with another metal makes it sturdier. However, alloys do not resist tarnish as well as pure gold. Different alloys change the color of the product. Gold may have tints of white, pink, peach, green, or black because of the alloy metals. The Black Hills of South Dakota is known for this type of jewelry. Black Hills gold jewelry often features flower or grapevine designs. The grapes are made of yellow gold, while the leaves are green and pink. Gold is alloyed with silver to produce the green, and with copper to produce the pink.

lubricant. Regular lubricants would evaporate or break down in the extreme conditions of space. So much gold is used in spacecraft that the *Columbia* space shuttle reportedly contained approximately 90 pounds (41 kg) of gold.[3]

Gold in the Columbia space shuttle was used on electric contacts, among other things.

The Best Metal for the Job

All metals can conduct electricity, but some do so better than others. Pure silver is the best conductor, but it tarnishes easily, which can interfere with conductivity. Copper is nearly as good and is commonly used for many electrical purposes. Pure gold is the third-best conductor of electricity, approximately 70 percent as good as copper.[4] Gold is also more expensive than copper. Yet gold is often used because it is more resistant to damage through corrosion.

Gold has a long, sometimes violent history, and today the gold industry faces challenges and criticisms about its treatment of people and the land. Yet the world has become dependent on gold for uses no one could have imagined a century ago. As gold is used in exciting new ways, from industry to medicine, demand for gold is likely to grow. Can the gold industry meet that demand while respecting human rights and protecting the environment?

2 | THE AGE OF EXPLORATION

Gold has been popular for thousands of years. Chances are it was first discovered when someone noticed a shiny gold nugget. Because gold does not corrode, it became a symbol of power and immortality in many cultures. Over the centuries, people around the world learned how to work gold in various ways.

Gold is sometimes found within larger rock pieces or formations. When a rock formation contains enough valuable material to make it worth mining and processing the rock, the rock is called ore. A process of heating and melting, called smelting, can be used to separate the gold from the rest of the rock. The ancient Egyptians developed a process for smelting gold by 3600 BCE. Egyptian goldsmiths built smelting furnaces and used blowpipes made from fire-resistant clay to heat them.

Throughout the ancient world, people wore gold jewelry. They developed techniques to take advantage of how easy gold is to work. They beat gold into thin sheets called gold leaf. They decorated surfaces with small granules of gold, a technique called granulation. They engraved gold, carving designs into its surface. They also molded pieces of gold

Ancient Egyptians crafted gold into ornate objects, including coffins for royal figures.

The Challenge of Smelting

Smelting is not as simple as heating a gold-bearing ore. The ore must be heated to a very high temperature, because gold melts at 1,943 degrees Fahrenheit (1,062°C).[2] A closed, insulated furnace allows a fire to reach that extreme temperature. A quality fuel and the right amount of oxygen encourage high temperatures and the right chemical balance. Traditionally, the oxygen was regulated with a bellows, a mechanical device that blows air into the fire. A bellows has a one-way valve to draw in air from outside the furnace rather than circulating air within the furnace. In the past, determining and controlling the temperature inside the furnace was difficult. Today, modern methods use more advanced technology for consistent smelting.

into shapes. With a technique called filigree, gold is pulled into thin wires, which are then twisted into different designs. The Egyptians used this technique by 2500 BCE. In ancient Rome, gemstones with gold settings were popular. In South America, civilizations in what is now Peru also developed ways of working with gold. Metalworkers used sheet gold to make objects such as crowns, masks, and jewelry. They hammered the sheets of gold to form raised designs.

Eventually, gold was also used as money. People used gold coins in Asia Minor, or modern Turkey and Armenia, by the late 700s BCE. At first these coins were made of electrum, a naturally occurring mix of gold and silver. In the 500s BCE, the first pure gold coins with stamped images appeared. These coins are attributed to King Croesus of Lydia. He was so famous for his riches that the expression "rich as Croesus" came to refer to great wealth.[1] Later, other civilizations, including the Greek and Roman Empires, also began using gold coins.

People also made gold into many other objects, often with religious or political symbolism. Kings used gold crowns and scepters. Religious items such as ritual vessels, masks, and statues were made of gold. In some ancient civilizations, temples and tombs were decorated with gold. Sometimes, gold items were buried with the dead to show the deceased person's status. One famous example is the death mask of the Egyptian pharaoh Tutankhamen, which is covered in gold leaf.

NEW WORLD DISCOVERIES

As the demand for gold grew, people went to extreme lengths to get it. Explorer Christopher Columbus set sail in 1492 CE searching for a western route accessing the spices and gold of Asia. He stumbled upon the Americas instead. Soon, Spanish conquistadors set out to conquer the New World. They were not motivated exclusively by gold. However, finding riches was a factor, along with the desire to spread religion. As one conquistador wrote, "We came here to serve God and his majesty,

Gold Teeth

Gold has been used in dental work for more than 3,000 years. The Etruscans, who lived in what is now Italy, may have been the first to use it in this way. In the 600s BCE, the Etruscans used gold wire to hold animal teeth in place of people's missing teeth. It is thought that some rich Etruscan women had teeth removed so they could be fitted with false gold teeth. This was a display of status and wealth. Gold may also have been used to fill cavities in ancient times. Gold is easy to form into delicate shapes, does not corrode, and does not harm the body. These qualities make it a good choice for fillings. The first definite archaeological evidence for the use of gold as fillings is from a little more than 1,000 years ago. Gold was used in dentistry until the late 1970s. Some gold fillings are still used today, although alternatives are more common.

The "Science" of Alchemy

Gold's value has encouraged many attempts to create gold from other substances. The practice of trying to turn other metals into gold is part of alchemy. This practice developed separately in Egypt and China and later spread through the Middle East and Europe. Although alchemy is not considered a true science, it provided the beginnings of chemistry. Alchemists developed laboratory equipment and techniques through experimentation. They also contributed to society through their discoveries and inventions. For example, Chinese alchemists discovered gunpowder, which was first used in fireworks and later in weapons. While alchemy was an attempt to discover the secrets of nature, it became associated with magic. After the 1300s, alchemists were viewed as sorcerers and were persecuted. However, in the 1600s and 1700s, many well-known scientists practiced alchemy among other scientific pursuits.

to give light to those who were in darkness, and to get rich as all men desire to do."[3]

Enslaved Indians in the Caribbean pan for gold for the Spanish.

In their expeditions, conquistadors traveled great distances through difficult terrain, encountering new societies. In less than one century, they conquered the Aztecs of Mexico and the Incas of Peru. Francisco Xerez, who recorded the Spanish expedition that led to the fall of the Inca Empire, wrote, "When has it ever happened, either in ancient or modern times, that such amazing exploits have been achieved?"[4]

Meanwhile, the devastation brought by the outsiders could not have been worse for the native people. The Spanish enslaved many Indians from Mexico to Peru. Some native slaves were forced to labor in mines or work farmland for their owners. Other enslaved Indians were forced to carry goods or made to construct buildings and roads. Many Indians were shipped to slave markets in other

El Dorado

When Spanish explorers reached South America, they found Indians with gold and heard stories of even greater wealth. Supposedly, an Indian tribe lived high in the Andes Mountains. When a chief gained power, he held a ceremony during which precious jewels were thrown into a lake. The Spanish called this chief El Dorado, or "the gilded one." Later, the term was used for a mythical city of gold. The Spanish never found El Dorado, although they decided Lake Guatavita in Colombia was where the chief's ceremony took place. The Spanish found hundreds of pieces of gold along the lake's edge but could not reach the greater treasure that may or may not have existed in deeper water. Later treasure hunters tried to explore Lake Guatavita. Attempts to lower the water level failed, and many workers died. A British company finally drained the lake in the early 1900s. This expedition found some artifacts, including gold. The lake is now protected as a national park.

countries and sold. European diseases such as smallpox and measles wiped out tens of millions of Indians in the Americas. To replace this lost workforce, Europeans began the African slave trade. The destruction of native societies opened the way for European settlers. They moved to the Americas in increasingly large numbers, taking land from those Indians still remaining.

The horrors Indians suffered from the conquistadors led to ethical debates. A 1550 council in Valladolid, Spain, called by the king considered questions of human rights. Some argued that Indians were "natural slaves," who should be conquered and converted to Christianity. However, Bartolomé de las Casas, a Dominican friar and Spanish historian, claimed, "All the world is human."[5] He criticized the cruelties of the conquistadors and convinced the Spanish king, Charles V, to temporarily stop the conquests. Still, the drive for power and riches overcame ethics, and the conquests resumed.

While gold may have been a major motivating factor for these explorations, the long-term effects had an impact in many areas of society and history. The exchange between the continents brought new foods to Europe, including the potato, the turkey, chili peppers, and chocolate. Trade routes changed, people moved, and new countries emerged. For both good and bad, the search for gold irrevocably changed both the Old and New Worlds.

3 | THE RUSH FOR RICHES

Gold has been found on every continent except Antarctica, yet it is relatively rare. The estimated amount of gold ever mined worldwide is 168,000 short tons (152,000 metric tons).[1] While that is enough to fill 60 tractor-trailers, it is a relatively small amount for thousands of years of worldwide demand. In contrast, by some estimates more than ten times as much silver has been mined.

One major challenge for mining gold is identifying where it is. Throughout history, people have stumbled on gold deposits by accident. Over the years, some people figured out the best places to look for gold. Yet finding gold is not simple, because gold can be found in many types of rock and ore deposits. These deposits are found in different geologic environments. The area may have a variety of rock types, water features, and other variables.

There is still much to learn. Geologists are not even certain of how the gold gets into larger rock formations. They have several hypotheses, each of which may be true for different deposits. All the hypotheses involve geothermal heat, either through hot underground water systems or from hot magma deep in the earth.

Geologists study rock structures, weathering processes, and other criteria to try to determine how to find gold.

NUGGETS, FLAKES, AND VEINS

One way or another, gold works its way into less valuable surrounding rock.

Gold tends to concentrate to form two types of major deposits: lode and placer. Lode refers to the primary deposit, where the gold is embedded in large rock formations. Lode gold often runs in veins through the rock, along with quartz. Over time, the surrounding rock may erode through weathering. Gold, which is very resistant to weathering, is then washed out of the rock. It is carried downstream in particles of dust, flakes, or nuggets. These settle as placer deposits.

Placer deposits are usually the first signs found by gold prospectors, people who search for new gold deposits. They search streambeds, looking for accumulations of coarse sand and gravel. Gold is often found among "black sands," sand that is dark because it has a concentration of heavy minerals such as magnetite.[2] Miners benefit from one of gold's physical properties: its high density. Gold deposits are denser than the surrounding ore. Because of this difference in density, gold can be separated from the surrounding gravel, sand, clay, or silt through gravity. Simple devices such as the gold pan and artificial channels called sluices take advantage of this.

Heavy Metal

The weight of gold is measured in troy ounces. A troy ounce is equal to 31.1034768 grams, slightly larger than a standard ounce.[3] This system is a holdover from a Roman system and is used only to measure gold, silver, platinum, and gunpowder. By maintaining this system worldwide over time, the value of these important commodities retains a single standard.

How a Sluice Box Works

Gold has a higher density than most other materials in a streambed. A sluice box allows the lighter materials to flow away, while the higher density gold sinks. The sluice box contains obstructions, called riffles, every few inches. Water flows over the riffles, which are designed to create swirls of water and suspended particles. The higher density gold particles sink, usually within the first few riffles. They can be retrieved later. The water and lighter particles eventually flow down and out of the sluice box.

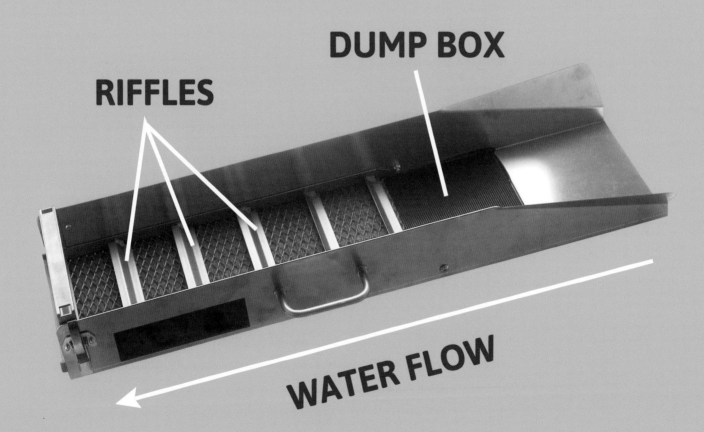

DUMP BOX

RIFFLES

WATER FLOW

Most of the gold is typically collected quickly with placer deposits. In contrast, a lode may contain large amounts of gold that can be worked for years. However, veins of gold running through rocks can be hard to find. To find a lode of gold, prospectors might first find placer gold and then follow the streambed, hoping to uncover the lode source. Finding the lode brings new challenges. The gold is embedded in other rock, so it must be crushed and separated. This requires expensive heavy equipment.

THE GREAT GOLD RUSHES

In the United States, miners first found rich gold deposits in the West. Sometimes a discovery set off a gold rush, where thousands of people hurried to the area to prospect. Most of those latecomers hoped to get rich quickly but instead found hard work with little or no payoff.

Although few individuals benefited personally from the gold rushes, the activity had a major effect on US history. For example, in 1848, carpenter James W. Marshall was working in the territory of

Panning for Gold

In gold panning, a prospector starts by finding a river or other waterway that is likely to contain gold. The prospector first strains the sediment in the riverbed. This is typically a mixture of silt, sand, and gravel. The prospector passes it through a sieve to remove rocks, checking to make sure none of them are gold nuggets. The prospector then scoops the remaining sediment into a pan with some water. The goal is to get the heavy particles of gold to settle to the bottom of the pan. To do this, the prospector vigorously shakes or swirls the pan. Heavy material such as gold settles to the bottom. Less valuable, lighter material rises to the top and can be rinsed out. The process is repeated multiple times until only the heaviest material remains. This should be black sand—and hopefully a bit of gold.

California. He was helping build a water-powered sawmill for a pioneer named John Sutter at the base of the Sierra Nevada mountains.

Marshall found shining flakes while working in the river. He later said, "It made my heart thump, for I was certain it was gold."[4] Marshall and Sutter tried to keep the discovery secret, but word quickly spread, and newspapers began covering the story. Several months later, 4,000 miners flocked to the area. People arrived by boat from Oregon, Mexico, Chile, Peru, and China. Once the news reports reached the East Coast in 1849, even more people headed to California. These hopeful miners became known as the '49ers. They had left their homes and families for a chance to become rich by striking gold in California.

Gold Hunting Hobbyists

Today, hobbyist gold hunters often look for placer deposits. The best experts can make good money through placer mining. Other people use it as an excuse to enjoy the outdoors, try something fun, and perhaps occasionally have the excitement of finding gold. People who want to find placer deposits may look for areas downstream from large gold mines of the past. Some prospectors also explore abandoned mines and the areas around them. However, this is often dangerous, and it requires landowner permission. Some mines may have tailings—waste rock from the mine—that still contain some gold. The rock may have been previously dismissed as having too little gold to make extracting it financially worthwhile. Modern equipment may make it possible to retrieve small amounts of gold from these rocks. Some gold is found in such small amounts that it takes laboratory analysis to reveal it. In these circumstances, it might be impossible to retrieve the gold without the financial backing of a large company.

Many '49ers spent their life savings to reach California, a difficult journey that took months.

More miners had to work for companies rather than prospecting on their own.

The United States had occupied California at the end of the Mexican-American War (1846–1848). At that time, approximately 150,000 American Indians lived in what is now California. The population also included 6,500 people of Spanish or Mexican descent and 700 others, primarily Americans. The non-native population of California grew to 100,000 people by the end of 1849.[5] San Francisco became a major city, while new towns popped up elsewhere. This large increase in population sped up the process of making California a state in 1850. Gold mining reached its peak in 1852 before declining, but settlers continued to arrive in California. The state's non-native population reached 380,000 people by the end of the decade.[6] Many of those who profited from the gold rush were not the miners themselves. Rather, the money went to the people who provided the miners with tools, food, lodging, and much more.

Around the World

A series of gold rushes hit New Zealand starting in the 1860s. As in the United States, few people became rich. Still, the discoveries brought many people to the young colony, including migrants from China. The gold that was found helped the economy. Australia also saw many gold rushes in the 1800s. Gold was often found in large nuggets rather than the small flakes and dust that were more common in North America. One gold nugget found in Australia weighed more than 200 pounds (91 kg).[7] A gold rush in South Africa in 1886 led to the establishment of Johannesburg, which is now the biggest city in the country. The gold in South Africa could be retrieved only with large equipment. This meant individual prospectors were quickly replaced with large mining companies. Some of these mining operations are still in business, along with newer mining companies.

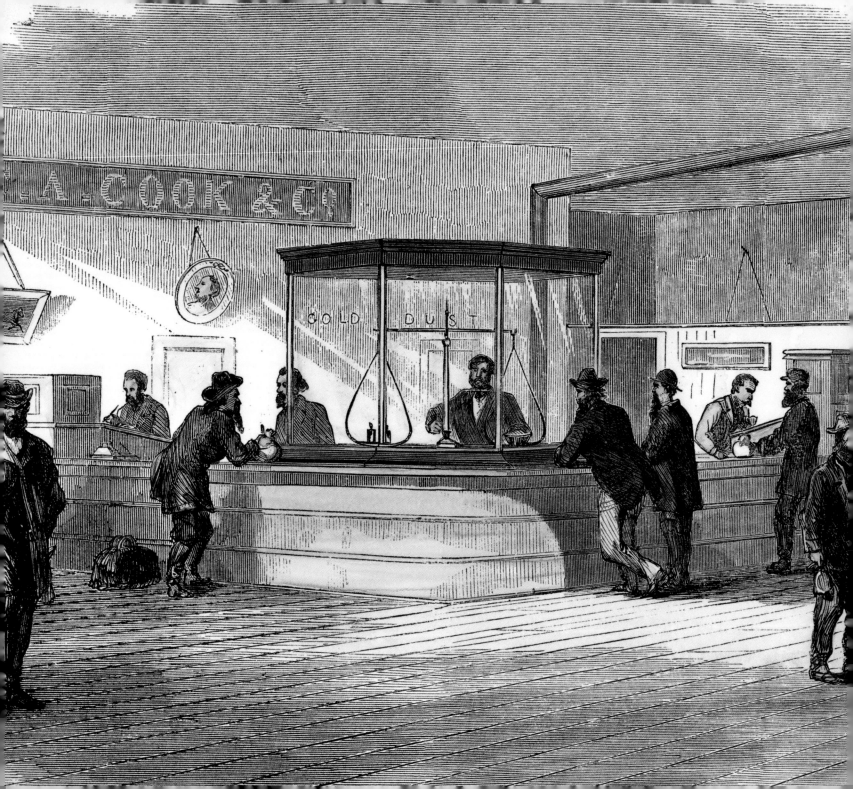

Many people settled permanently, and Denver became an important city in the region, opening banks and other establishments.

Many native cultures were destroyed by the influx of new settlers. Miners and other settlers took over native lands. Some miners murdered local American Indians, viewing them as potential competitors for the gold. The new immigrants also brought diseases that killed many natives. By some estimates, only approximately 10 percent of the American Indians in California survived the gold rush years.[8]

The search for gold was also an important factor in bringing settlers to other parts of the West. Gold brought the first permanent white settlers to Idaho and led to the establishment of the Idaho Territory in 1863. Some hopeful prospectors spread throughout the Western United States looking for areas they thought might contain gold. Their discoveries led to the founding of new cities. For example, in 1858, a group of prospectors found gold in Colorado, near what is today Denver. This brought in some prospectors, who then discovered several other Colorado gold lodes. By some estimates, up to 100,000 people headed to Colorado looking for gold in 1859.[9] As in California, American Indians often suffered when new settlers arrived.

Value in the Rocks

In some cases, mining gold is less lucrative than mining other minerals, such as silver, lead, and zinc. According to the US Bureau of Mines, Idaho has more mineable gold than any other state. Yet Idaho produces very little gold, with most mines focused on other minerals. Silver and phosphate are the two primary minerals mined in Idaho. Industrial minerals may bring in more money now than precious metals do. Industrial minerals include sand and gravel used for roads, phosphate used to make fertilizer and other chemicals, and many more.

Cities such as Dawson grew as more settlers arrived in search of gold.

STRIKING IT RICH

Other gold rushes followed. One began in 1896, near Dawson, in the Yukon Territory of Canada. The local people who first found gold became rich. The Yukon region of Canada was so remote that word spread slowly at that time. Eleven months after the first discovery, a steamship from Dawson reached Seattle, Washington. A Seattle newspaper reported "more than a ton of gold" on the ship, setting off the Klondike gold rush. Approximately 100,000 people headed to the Yukon in the next six months, but only 30,000 people completed the trip.[10] They had to walk most of the way, carrying a year's worth of supplies—hundreds of pounds—on sleds or pack animals. Many people died from starvation or cold, or they gave up. Those who did make it found that all the potential gold-bearing land had already been claimed. These latecomers had to work for others. Still, this gold rush brought many people north. Those seeking gold were mostly men, but women also arrived to run hotels, dance halls, and other businesses.

Most early prospectors made little money, even if they managed to stake a mining claim. Sifting a pan of gold to wash out the sand and gravel takes five to ten minutes. It may reveal only a few pennies' worth of gold. Most early miners made a few dollars a day, if that. While some gave up when the easy gold ran out, others turned to more serious mining, using machinery. As mining industrialized, it required expensive equipment.

The lust for gold was a major factor in the exploration and colonization of the West. The United States, Canada, and other countries changed dramatically because of the search for gold.

4 | NEW MINING METHODS

After the easily accessible gold ran out during the 1849 California gold rush, new techniques improved production. In the Sierra Nevada mountains, large quantities of placer gold were found in river gravel deposits. In areas with plenty of surface water, the most cost-effective way to recover large amounts of gold used water cannons, or high-pressure hoses. These machines broke apart the placer ores and washed away the sand and gravel. This created a semiliquid mixture of rock and water, called slurry. The strong stream of water directed the slurry through sluices. Then the hoses were turned off so the miners could collect gold where it had gathered at the bottom of the sluices. This required much less labor to process more rock.

This form of mining, called hydraulic mining, was eventually abandoned. It left behind 5,000 miles (8,000 km) of waterways on the west slope of the Sierra Nevada mountains.[1] Many of these reservoirs and canals were later used for hydroelectric power systems. However, hydraulic mining had also left behind serious environmental damage. The system had removed entire ridges and hillsides. Forests were destroyed, and the massive movement of debris through sluices and tunnels caused flooding in the farmlands below. Some farms were buried

Miners in the late 1800s constructed tunnels to control the slurry, and they built reservoirs, flumes, and ditches to bring water to the mines.

Grown or Mined

A common statement among geologists and the mining industry is, "If it can't be grown, it has to be mined."[2] This makes the point that many familiar objects contain materials that came out of the ground in some form. For example, cement cinder blocks in walls, the gasoline that powers cars, and the plastic packaging around food are made from materials that had to be extracted from the ground. This makes mining, and the manufacturing that turns those raw ingredients into finished products, necessary to keep the country running and people employed.

under the millions of cubic feet of waste rock that ran down the mountain valleys. Hydraulic mining created huge profits for companies, but enormous damage was done to the landscape. And the damage did not end there.

This NASA image shows how land in California was damaged from mining operations in the 1800s.

DEADLY POISONS

Gold was also removed from the surrounding rock through chemical processes. In hydraulic mining, gold particles were often recovered from sluices by adding liquid mercury. When gold and mercury met, the gold dissolved into the mercury, and formed an amalgam, or compound. Mercury has a high density, so the gold-mercury amalgam sunk while the sand and gravel washed out. This process allowed the miners to collect very small particles of gold. In the 1800s, the mercury was heated until it vaporized, leaving behind the gold. With later methods, the mercury was recycled.

However, in 1800s hydraulic mining, between 10 and 30 percent of this mercury was lost into the environment, poisoning many sites. An estimated 10 million pounds (4.5 million kg) of mercury

The Cyanide Code

Multiple groups developed safety rules regarding cyanide. Government agencies, nongovernmental organizations, and the mining industry participated, with involvement from the United Nations Environment Program. It is called the International Cyanide Management Code For the Manufacture, Transport, and Use of Cyanide in the Production of Gold. The code details how companies should safely use cyanide. The intent is to protect human health and reduce environmental impact. Companies that adopt the code have their methods audited in order to reach certification. However, the program is voluntary, so gold mining companies are not required to participate.

was released into the environment through placer mining operations in California.[3] Mercury was widely used in mining operations until the early 1960s. In some watersheds, enough mercury is concentrated to still pose a risk to human health. Mercury is a neurotoxin that damages the nervous system. It can cause many problems, especially in children, including seizures, problems with coordination, and mental impairment.

Mining operations continued to develop new techniques to more efficiently remove gold from rock. Many of these methods used heavy equipment, chemical processes, or both. One process for recovering gold from low-grade ore involves dissolving gold in a mixture of chemicals including cyanide. This cyanide process has been used since the 1890s and is still widely used. While cyanide is used in many industries, and proponents claim it can be used safely, it is highly toxic. Cyanide wastewater is hazardous to wildlife if not properly managed. Accidental spills have wiped out fish and other aquatic animals in nearby bodies of water. Wastewater from mines may also

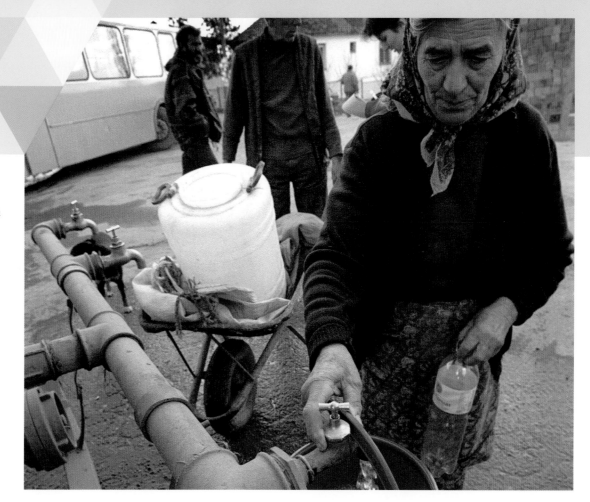

A cyanide spill originating in Romania in 2000 forced neighboring cities and countries to disconnect their water systems.

contain other poisons, such as arsenic. Today, most governments worldwide regulate the use of cyanide in large amounts. This helps reduce the amount used and avoid accidental spills.

GOLD'S UPS AND DOWNS

Advances in mining methods such as these made gold recovery practical mainly for governments and companies with money, staff, and equipment. This helped transform gold mining into a big

Fort Knox

In the United States, the Fort Knox Bullion Depository contains much of the country's gold reserves. The depository is southwest of Louisville, Kentucky. The gold there is in the form of bars. They are approximately the size of building bricks. Each bar weighs approximately 400 troy ounces, or 27.5 pounds (12.5 kg).[5] Fort Knox has held gold since 1937. In the 1930s, President Franklin D. Roosevelt passed an executive order requiring Americans to sell their gold coins to the Federal Reserve in exchange for paper money. Most of these coins were melted and formed into gold bars. This greatly increased the gold reserves held by the United States as a guarantee that US currency would remain valuable. Fort Knox was built to store much of this gold. Visitors are not permitted at Fort Knox. The gold vaults are never opened except for rare audits.

business dominated by large companies. However, gold production in the United States had its ups and downs in the 1900s. Prospecting by individuals increased in the 1930s, during the Great Depression. With many people out of work, searching for placer gold was a low-cost option for someone trying to earn money. However, few people struck it rich. Then the US government shut down most large US mining operations during World War II (1939–1945). After the war, the price of gold, set by the US government at $35 per ounce, was not high enough to make reopening most mines worthwhile.[4]

As with many countries, the United States was on a gold standard for many years. A gold standard is a money system in which the value of currency is linked to a specific quantity of gold. The United Kingdom instituted the first gold standard in 1821. Before that, silver was the principal metal used for money worldwide. The United States and many other countries adopted a gold standard in the 1870s. In addition, many contracts required the debtor to repay the creditor in gold dollars. Factors such as these kept up the demand for gold, and thus the price. In 1933, the United States went off the gold standard. Around the world, the specifics of the gold standard varied over the years, with each country's government often exerting some control on price. The international money system is now based on paper currency, so gold has become less important in world finances.

In 1971, the United States deregulated gold, meaning the government stopped controlling its price. Gold's value rose sharply, reaching more than $600 per ounce by 1980.[6] This encouraged both experts and amateurs to search for gold. Several US mines reopened. They used new technology to process low-grade deposits, ore that had been ignored in the past because it contained such small quantities of gold.

How to Talk about Gold

The degree of purity in gold can vary greatly. Several terms are used to describe the level of purity. The term *fineness* defines how much actual gold a piece of natural or refined gold contains. For example, a gold nugget that is "880-fine" contains 88 percent pure gold, and 12 percent other metal.[7]

In jewelry, the term *karat* is more often used. Karat describes the amount of gold in an object, based on a total of 24 parts. Pure gold is called 24 karat gold, while an alloy that is only 50 percent gold by weight is called 12 karat gold.[8] 14 karat gold is often used in jewelry. This means the jewelry has 14 parts of gold and 10 parts of other metals.[9] In chemistry, gold is identified by the symbol Au, from the Latin *aurum*, which means "shining dawn."[10]

5 | BECOMING BIG BUSINESS

Much of the United States and the rest of the developed world has been searched for gold in the last two centuries. Most gold that is easily accessible in high concentrations has already been found. One forecast suggests the amount of gold that can be retrieved through current methods will drop substantially after 2030, if demand continues at the current rate. Mining companies must improve their technology to keep producing gold at a reasonable cost.

New technology has already changed the gold business in many ways. The methods are most practical for large businesses because of the heavy equipment and labor they require. In the United States, 97 percent of all metals are mined through open-pit mining.[1] In open-pit mining, gold ore is crushed into gravel, placed in special piles, and sprinkled with a chemical solution. This process dissolves any gold or copper, which slowly filters to the bottom of the heap. It is then collected and processed. This system is known as heap leaching.

Because it is successful in many geographic conditions, heap leaching has been growing in recent decades. In 2014, approximately 150 major gold-silver mines worldwide

Modern mining methods allow more gold to be extracted from some ores than in the past.

Ore is removed from underground mines by trucks or rail carts.

used heap leaching.[2] The process can also be used to extract metals from abandoned mine tailings. Open-pit mining is less expensive than underground mining, so rock with a lower grade can be mined using open-pit methods where it would be uneconomic to mine using underground methods. However, the process is still expensive enough that gold prices must remain high to make it lucrative.

Underground mining is still the best method for retrieving gold from some ores. In underground mines, shafts are excavated deep into the earth in order to reach the ore. The tunnels may be drilled or blasted out of the rock. Once the ore is removed, it is processed in a similar way to open-pit mining.

Mining success is affected by the recovery rates for metals. This describes the percentage

Some underdeveloped countries still use old mining techniques.

of valuable material that can be refined out of ore. Mineral recovery rates have increased greatly in the last century. Recovering more gold from ore makes a mine more profitable. Transportation is also easier and cheaper than in the days when ore had to be transported from remote areas in wagons.

KEEPING MINERS SAFER

Many other technology advances are underway. These improvements are also likely to increase the need for mining industry employees with engineering degrees while reducing the need for less skilled workers in more dangerous jobs. For example, some mining operations are experimenting with automated trucks, railways, and drilling systems. These systems are controlled remotely via computers rather than through direct human contact. Automated systems are typically more accurate and efficient. They are also safer because they reduce human error and keep human operators away from dangerous areas, such as open pits. In addition, technology can

Land Rules for Gold Hunting

People who are interested in searching for gold, whether professionally or as a hobby, must understand the laws. To enter private land, they must get permission from the landowner. Ownership is not always obvious in remote areas. Some public lands are open to prospecting and mining, but not all. Those that allow mineral operations have rules and regulations governing access and use. The US Bureau of Land Management offers advice and maps to help people find suitable areas for prospecting. Once a valuable mineral is found, the discoverer can then stake a claim to continue working the area.

Large companies rather than individual prospectors now dominate the gold business.

operate 24 hours a day, with one operator supervising several machines. These changes will likely eliminate many low-skilled jobs but increase the need for trained workers.

Other new technologies make it easier to reach gold deposits underground. Reef boring can drill small tunnels throughout a gold deposit. These holes are then filled with a solution that turns as hard as rock. Additional ore can then be removed from around the area. The rock-hard deposits stabilize the mine while allowing the majority of gold ore to be removed. The process is much faster than traditional methods and can be used in areas that are too dangerous for human miners. It could also allow a mine to operate for an additional 30 years by accessing gold ore that could not have been retrieved by traditional methods.

Future technology could help mining operations to extract other hard-to-reach gold. A Dutch company called Damen Shipyards Group is developing robotic equipment to mine for minerals underwater. A US company, Shackleton Energy, is working with a Norwegian-based company, Zaptec, to explore the possibility of drilling on the moon. They are also developing a plasma drilling technology. Originally used in the oil and gas industry, plasma drilling uses high temperatures to cut through rock. Shackleton and Zaptec hope this technology can be altered to help extract water and minerals from the moon.

Demand for Gold

Gold prices change based on demand, which stems from a variety of factors. In 2001, gold was $260 per troy ounce. It hit $1921.15 in 2011.[3]

Gold Price Adjusted for Inflation

Dollars per troy ounce

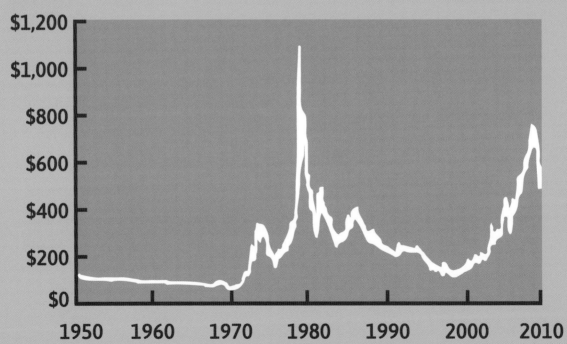

Local Guatemalans protest a Goldcorp mine over concerns about pollution and claims the local mine had not brought in the benefits that had been promised.

controlled. Even the rock itself can undergo a chemical reaction when pulled out of the ground and exposed to air. Gold and other metals are sometimes found in underground ores that contain a lot of sulfide minerals. When the sulfide is exposed to air and water, it creates sulfuric acid. In high enough concentrations, this corrosive substance can kill all living things. This can contaminate nearby water and plants. Environmental regulations are designed to protect the land and water, and all the people and animals that live in the area.

In countries that are politically stable and safe, most major gold deposits have already been exploited. That means mining companies often do business in less stable countries. If a civil war or other crisis breaks out, the company may lose the business. A gold mine cannot be moved to a safer location. Big businesses from outside a country may also face animosity within the country. Local people may resent the gold being removed from their country and sometimes file lawsuits. Factors such as these mean that big companies may now dominate the gold industry, but they do not necessarily have an easy business. In Guatemala, Goldcorp Inc. faced backlash against plans to expand its mining operation in 2007. Local people claimed they had not benefited enough from the existing mines. In 2014, public complaints over pollution in Colombia caused the government to crack down on mining companies. Planned gold mines from AngloGold Ashanti and Eco Oro were delayed. The Colombian mining minister said mining companies should work for approval from the communities along with their official permits. While community approval is not an official requirement, without it, most projects fail.

6 | ECONOMIC EFFECTS

A large gold mine can produce millions or even billions of dollars and employ hundreds or thousands of workers. That means each major gold mine has a strong effect on the local economy. But is this effect primarily positive or primarily negative? The answer may depend on the company, local circumstances, and even on personal opinion.

Large gold mining companies typically have corporate headquarters in one country and mines in several other countries. Most mining companies are based in developed countries. For example, as of 2013, more than half of the world's publicly listed exploration and mining companies were headquartered in Canada. Those companies had operations in more than 100 other countries.[1] Sometimes working between countries results in ethical dilemmas. Developing countries may not have the same pay rates, standards for workplace health and safety, and environmental regulations as developed countries. Some companies may be tempted to take advantage of this discrepancy. They could save money by paying foreign workers poorly and ignoring proper safety procedures and environmental dangers. However, that could lead to protests that hurt the company's reputation.

Many gold mines are in developing countries that are not highly industrialized and have a low standard of living.

The Super Pit in Australia is the country's largest open mine and is partially owned by Barrick Gold.

BARRICK GOLD

Barrick Gold is the world's largest gold producer. The company is based in Toronto, Canada, and has mines in Africa, Australia, and the Americas. More than 75 percent of the company's gold production comes from Argentina, Chile, Peru, the United States, and Canada.[2] A new mining operation in Nevada is expected to start construction in 2020, joining several existing mines in that state. The $1 billion project is predicted to produce 440,000 ounces (12 million g) of gold each year. Overall, Barrick Gold hopes to produce at least 4.5 million ounces (128 million g) of gold each year through 2020.[3] Barrick employs more than 17,000 people around the world. The company states, "At Barrick, our vision is the generation of wealth through responsible mining—wealth for our owners, our people, and the countries and communities with which we partner." Peter Munk founded Barrick Gold in 1983.[4] A Canadian, Munk graduated with a degree in electrical engineering from the University of Toronto. His company grew quickly, becoming an industry leader within 25 years.

ILLEGAL MINES

In many cases, large companies may do a better job of respecting human rights and the environment than smaller local companies. The latter may not follow international standards and may not even be licensed by the local country's government. In Ghana, thousands of children work dangerous jobs in unlicensed mines. The children—usually ages 15 to 17 but sometimes as young as 9 years old—suffer serious health risks. The mercury used to process gold ore can cause brain damage and other disabilities. Children have been injured and even killed in mine collapses. Gold from these mines gets sold along a chain that eventually takes it to businesses such as banks and jewelry companies. First, local traders buy gold from these small mining operations. The gold may pass between several trading companies until it reaches international gold refiners. The gold refinery purifies the gold, removing any other metals. From there, the gold may be sold to the makers of jewelry, electronics,

Artisanal Miners

While big companies dominate the gold mining industry, most of the individual miners in the world do not work for any company. These people are known as artisanal or small-scale miners. They typically pan for gold or use hand tools rather than machinery. They are not protected by labor or safety regulations that apply to employees at businesses. For many of these people, gold mining is their best way to make a living. However, they are at risk for accidents and health problems. They are vulnerable to abusive practices from the people who buy their gold. They may ignore environmental regulations, if they even know about them, contributing to environmental damage. At any given time, there are 15 million artisanal gold miners, and up to 40 million when gold prices are high.[5] They mainly work in developing countries.

Peruvian police set fire to an illegal mining operation.

or other products all over the world. Companies must study every stage of their supply chains to make sure no gold is coming from unethical sources, such as those that utilize child labor. Yet some companies prefer to look the other way.

In Peru, approximately 30,000 people work illegally in gold mines in the Amazon rain forest.[6] Even children work at the mines there, often as service workers in kitchens. Most child workers are orphans or were sold into labor. Illegal mining is dangerous because no safety regulations are followed. In one Peruvian mining area, approximately four men die each week from pit cave-ins or other accidents. The miners may also be directly exposed to toxic substances such as mercury. Yet the work is still tempting, because a good day can pay more than working for a month at a legal job in town. One miner, 20 years old, noted, "We work at least 18 hours a day. But you can make a lot of money. In another few years, if nothing happens to me, I can go back to my town, buy a nice house, buy a shop, work simply and relax for my life."[7]

Another Peruvian miner, asked if his job was good, replied, "No, but I have raised five children in this way. Two work in tourism. One is an accountant. Another has just finished business school and another is in business school. My children have moved past a job like this."[8]

Consumers may hesitate to buy products made in developing countries, as a way to protest poor ethical practices. Yet reducing the supply of products such as gold from developing countries can increase poverty there. The increasing poverty can then encourage even worse business practices and more illegal mining. According to the World Gold Council, a market development organization for the gold industry, "it is important that international and domestic business, governments, civil society, and consumers all play their part in raising standards and encouraging responsible global trade."[9] That means big businesses must commit to following the best practices for human rights, workplace safety, and environmental protection. Companies should follow

Mining companies often bring good changes to areas too, including jobs and facilities for locals.

international standards, even if those standards are stricter than a specific country's laws.

DEALING WITH DOWNTURNS

Today, local unions may negotiate wages and benefits for mining employees around the world. Mining companies sometimes provide medical benefits to employees. Mining companies have also supported local communities with a variety of development and social programs. These can include infrastructure development. For example, a mining company may build roads and bridges and establish power, water supply, and sewage systems. Companies may also provide funds for building community centers, health clinics, daycare centers, and schools. Some offer scholarships for local students to attend school. They might develop training programs to help young people prepare for working in mining.

A Healthy Mind

Mental health can be a concern in any population, but mining involves some challenges that add mental stress. Miners often have to work in harsh climates and remote locations, away from the typical comforts of civilization. Sometimes workers are flown in to the worksite for temporary shifts, which means leaving their families for weeks at a time. An Australian study found that employees working under this method had a higher rate of mental health problems—30 percent versus a national average of 20 percent among the general public.[11] Some companies are participating in studies of worker mental health and are trying to find ways to improve the system. Answers can include revised work schedules, identifying problems earlier, and counseling services.

In some cases, programs may continue even after a mine has closed.

Companies might also invest in local programs to help the economy in ways not directly related to mining. AngloGold Ashanti, a company with headquarters in South Africa and mines in at least nine countries, operates a mine near Cajamarca, Peru. The company started a joint project with the local community and the Peruvian government aimed to help the local cattle ranching industry. The project established a breeding program and helped eliminate two diseases affecting cattle. This allowed area ranchers to sell more meat.

But supporting local communities can be expensive. Mining has suffered from an economic downturn in recent years. As of October 2015, approximately 10 percent of global gold mines were running at a loss.[10] Large companies in any industry respond to hard times by cutting costs. Some are tempted to do so by firing workers, reducing pay, and not upgrading equipment. However, in a report on 2016 mining industry trends, the advisory group Deloitte warned mining companies about this practice. Although 40 to 50 percent of most mining costs come from labor, firing workers and cutting payment leads to backlash.[12] This could mean union strikes that close down a mine, anger from local communities, and even violence. In addition, with the loss of experienced workers, knowledge is lost. All of these effects from cutting costs could further hurt the company's income.

Deloitte recommended that mining companies start honest discussions with workers and governments, trying to find a solution that works best. This might mean cutting some jobs but helping those employees find new training opportunities. It could mean increasing wages when there is an increase in productivity. Maintaining health clinics and schools may be worthwhile because of the positive effect on community relations. Schools and clinics also help produce an educated workforce and keep it healthy.

Respecting Local Culture

In the United States and Canada, gold mining companies may operate on land owned by American Indian or First Nation tribes. Negotiations between company and tribal representatives determine how a mine may operate. Results may include setting the number of employees that must be hired from the tribe, establishing training programs for young people, and other community development. Ideally, this benefits both the mining company and local people. Chief Rodney Mark of the Cree Nation of Wemindji from northern Quebec, Canada, participated in negotiations with Goldcorp for a local mine. The partnership established training programs to help Cree tribal members find employment at the mine. "This will take a bit of a lifestyle change because much time here is spent hunting and fishing," Chief Mark said. "But once people realize the variety of jobs, the salaries and the shift flexibility—two weeks of work and two weeks off—they will see that it fits their lifestyle well."[13]

FINDING BALANCE

Finding a balance between the competing demands of government, industry, and local needs is not easy. In some countries, local citizens tend to see mining companies as foreign-owned monsters trying to steal the resources and exploit local workers. Environmental groups often protest the damage mines can do to nature. Activists from inside and outside the country may try to prevent new mining operations or close existing mines. Meanwhile, governments want the largest amount of money in terms of fees and taxes. Mining companies also receive pressure from shareholders, who expect a good return on their investment. Pleasing all of these parties is nearly impossible. A wrong step could lead to strikes, protests, or even violent riots.

Recent years have seen greater awareness and respect for the rights of local residents, along with more concern for the environment. The mining industry is still learning how to adapt to current ethical standards, which continuously change. Companies that are members of the International Council on Mining and Metals are required to follow the Sustainable Development Framework. These principles cover ethical business practices. They attempt to balance human rights, environmental protection, and local economic benefits with bringing in the income needed to support the company and its investors.

However, that process is not simple. People may disagree strongly about whether the benefits gold mines bring are worthwhile. In an interview with the *Economist*, former Barrick Gold chairman Peter Munk described one challenge his company faced:

In Chile we fought our way through years of approvals at unbelievable cost. The lawyers for this splinter group went to the constitutional court and claimed we still shouldn't be allowed to mine because the constitution guaranteed the unimpeded right of indigenous groups to their customary lifestyle. And the very fact that the mine was approved will change their ability to fish, their ability [to] hunt, ability to graze, to walk. There are 170 of them. And maybe they cannot graze, which I fully admit. But they are endangering 3,000 people's jobs and huge economic benefits to the community, educational benefits, tax benefits, foreign exchange benefits.[14]

This brings up the questions: Which group is more important? Who should decide? "Diverse economies have been built on the back of gold," said Terry Heymann, then with the World Gold Council. "There is a responsibility for everyone to move forward, but that can be very hard in a world of immediate results and quarterly earnings."[15]

Creating Jobs

The World Gold Council offers statistics on gold's impact on the global economy. The organization claims gold mining provided more than 500,000 jobs at gold mines in the top 15 gold-producing countries in the world, as of 2012.[16] For each job at a gold mine, up to ten additional jobs may be created in the local community. For example, a new gold mining town needs people to build roads and buildings. More workers are needed to supply and run shops in the town. In the countries that produce and buy the most gold, gold contributed an estimated $210 billion to the economy. Approximately $78 billion came from large-scale commercial gold mines.[17]

7 | PROTECTING PEOPLE

Gold mining companies may find themselves embroiled in conflicts that have nothing directly to do with the gold business. Gold is one of the products that are associated with providing funding for armed conflict. Gold is fairly easy to smuggle, making it appealing to armed groups. Gold smugglers in some African countries pay violent groups a percentage of the trade. Gold that contributes to armed conflict is known as conflict gold.

International companies involved in the gold industry may inadvertently contribute to these illegal and unethical activities. A process known as due diligence can help prevent abuses. Due diligence requires companies to carry out checks on their supply chains. Companies should look for any evidence that they may be causing harm through their activities. In 2010, the United States passed legislation known as the Dodd-Frank Wall Street Reform and Consumer Protection Act. It requires companies listed in the United States to carry out due diligence on minerals sourced from some African countries. However, companies based in other countries may not be subject to similar laws.

Violent groups searching for gold have been responsible for rapes, murders, and forcing thousands of people to flee their homes.

Recycling Gold

All of the gold that has ever been found is still in existence, although it may be trapped in a discarded cell phone in a city dump. Gold is ideal for recycling. It can be melted down and reused over and over. This is an advantage for maintaining the world's gold supply. However, it makes it hard to track the original source of gold. Some "conflict gold"—gold that has helped fund armed conflict—could work its way into the system through recycling. Due diligence at every step of the supply chain can reduce this problem.

The gold mining industry as a whole has also established policies intended to maintain the gold supply while protecting human rights. The Conflict-Free Gold Standard was developed by the World Gold Council to help this process. It is intended to ensure companies do not "cause, support or benefit unlawful armed conflict, or contribute to human rights abuses or breaches of international humanitarian law."[1] To be effective, the standard must be followed through all parts of the gold industry. It should be in place from the mines and refineries to the markets where pure gold is bought and sold and to final manufacturers such as jewelry companies.

In addition, most gold mining companies have their own official policies on human rights. These companies recognize these policies are important for their reputation as well as for maintaining ethical standards. When company oversight ensures that all employees, in every location, follow the policies, human rights abuses can be avoided.

Compliance to the Conflict-Free Gold Standard is voluntary. Whether it is followed varies between companies and from country to country. At a 2013 meeting discussing progress, Louise

Arimatsu, an international lawyer, noted, "The good guys are concerned about reputations. They are already complying."[2] But other companies were resisting the standards. When jewelry companies and other gold buyers demand gold produced by ethical standards, companies are encouraged to improve their practices.

The gold industry can set and follow standards for best practices. The general public can pressure all companies to do their best. Consumers can help by buying from responsible companies. When all parts of the system work together, abuses can be prevented.

HUMAN RIGHTS IN DANGER

Current laws, regulations, and industry standards have reduced mining company abuses. Still, there are always exceptions. International companies have been accused of violating local laws and human rights. This can lead to complicated legal action. For example, Hudbay Minerals, a company

Tech Protections

Mining workers face unusual risks compared to people in many industries. Some companies operate in countries where a portion of the local population may be hostile toward the company. This can result in kidnappings and even murder. Some mining companies now embed tracking devices and panic buttons into the mobile phones or laptops of their workers. This allows an endangered worker to alert the company immediately in case of a problem. The tracking device makes it easier to find that person. Other security measures include fences, guards, and cameras around facilities. Instead of standard ID cards, some companies use cards with advanced technology such as facial recognition. This helps prevent unauthorized people from accessing the mines or business offices.

Sometimes gold mining results in violent and deadly riots among miners and local people, including in Guatemala.

based in Canada, was accused of serious crimes in Guatemala. A Guatemalan woman claimed her husband was killed after he protested some mining practices. His killers poured gasoline over him, struck a match, and lit the gasoline. A formal complaint was filed, but local people hesitated to pursue the matter because, they said, they were threatened. The woman eventually took the case to the Canadian courts, but as of 2016 had not yet been resolved. Hudbay Minerals denies the allegations, claiming it "[does] not condone violence of any kind, against anyone."[3]

Wiping Out a Tribe

In Brazil, land designated to the Yanomami tribe has been overrun with illegal miners. They brought diseases that wiped out nearly 20 percent of the Yanomami population.[4] Poison from the mines has affected nearly the entire tribe. Brazil's environmental special forces have tried to shut down the mines, but it is hard to police the remote territory.

In another case, a woman claimed a group of police officers, soldiers, and mining security officials invaded her tiny Guatemalan village. She says the men took turns raping her and other women in the village. The men then set her home on fire, claiming the land belonged to the mine. The people in this region had been protesting the effects of mining activity. They complained about contaminated water sources, human malnutrition, skin diseases, livestock dying, and house walls cracking after shaking. They accused the mining company of bribing local authorities and issuing threats to protesters. Processes that would have protected local people, including an international treaty, had been ignored when the mine was allowed to set up business.

The Guatemalan woman sued Hudbay Minerals. At the time of the allegations, the mine was owned by a subsidiary of another Canadian company, Skye Resources Inc. Hudbay bought the mine in 2008 and has since sold the mine.

With the buying and selling, and with the companies based in another country, the legal situation is complex. Some countries exert oversight on the mining companies with headquarters in their borders, even when those companies are working in foreign countries. However, often the home country leaves the legal issues to the country where the accusations take place. Local governments and law enforcement may be understaffed, uninterested, or open to bribes. This can make it hard for people in those countries to get justice.

Human rights groups say they have tracked years of problems with mining companies. Complaints include forced labor, evicting local people from their homes, and attacking and sometimes killing protesters. Mining companies have also been accused of damaging the environment, including protected zones and nature reserves. These claims tended to be ignored by local courts, which are often corrupt and possibly paid off by the mining companies. The local people are often poorly educated and have little money to spend on legal action. Indigenous people may not speak the dominant language in their country, let alone in the country where the company is based.

CLOSED MINE, WAR ZONE

In some cases, communities become dependent on the mining industry for jobs and other support. Some mines have closed and quit supporting the local community, leaving tragedy in their wake. Blyvooruitzicht, a mine southwest of Johannesburg, closed in 2013 after 77 years of operation. The 6,000 residents of the town owned by the mine had benefited from jobs, clinics, and even a golf course. When the mine closed, 1,700 workers lost their jobs.[5] "We had murders, we had a mass rape, it was a real mess," said Pule Molefe, a former mine worker, in a *Bloomberg* article. "The municipality came in and cut off our water supply. They wanted to cut electricity also."[6]

Now two brothers are trying to reopen the mine. One of them, Dane Viljoen, has said, "We're young but we want to build a legacy, a good legacy. We want to be the guys that build libraries, put money into universities." However, opening the mine again will cost at least $10 million. Molefe remarked, "We hope they'll do what they say they're

Left Behind

South Africa was once the world's largest gold producer, but the industry has crashed in recent years. Because of this crash, between 2004 and 2015, a third of the gold industry's employees were fired, leaving 60,000 people out of work. Many kept mining illegally. The South African illegal miners may spend 24 hours underground and make $50 on a good day.[7] A bad day may pay only three dollars. The miners may use dynamite to open a hole and make a dangerous descent underground. They have no safety equipment, and the hoses that once delivered fresh air into the mine have fallen apart. The miners sell the material they retrieve to middlemen, who sell it to refiners. In this way, the gold works its way into the mainstream system.

Illegal miners and thieves overran Blyvooruitzicht and turned it into a war zone, according to the local community.

going to do. But we want to see action and jobs. Many people came to us with big promises but we've been let down many times."[8]

In any industry, unethical practices are possible. The risk for abuse is higher when big businesses work in remote areas of developing countries, where local people tend to be poor, uneducated, and powerless. Problems can be reduced when everyone works together to prevent them. For the gold industry, that includes the companies, industry organizations, governments, and consumers.

8 | DIGGING THE LAND

Human business activity will always release some level of pollution. This affects air quality, water systems, and local human and animal populations. Mining companies acknowledge these effects and typically have policies to address them. The mine, its buildings and other structures, and the roads leading to it affect the land and water. Open-pit mines move huge amounts of earth. By one estimate, it takes 20 short tons (18 metric tons) of rock to produce enough gold to make one ring.[1] The waste is discarded, and it may contain chemicals used to extract the gold from the ore. Erosion from mining operations can clog streams and rivers.

Companies must not only deal with waste from the mining processes, but with human waste as well. Because mines are often located in remote locations, garbage and sewage services are rarely available. The company usually manages its own sewage treatment facilities and landfills to handle waste produced at the site.

A mining company must often share resources with the local community. In some regions, there may not be enough water for both the mine and the local people. According to one

Most mining companies have policies in place to reduce pollution.

Energy is one of a company's biggest operating costs in running a gold mine.

report, more than half of the operations from the largest mining companies are located in countries with significant water stress. Governments may refuse water permits for new mines and have sometimes reduced the water rights they previously granted. Gold mining companies may try to reduce the amount of water they need by recycling water. If the water is reused within a closed-loop system, this can also reduce the risk of polluted water being released into the environment.

Mining operations need power for lights, ventilation, cooling systems, and equipment operation. This energy can compose up to 30 percent of a company's total operating costs.[2] Local communities cannot always provide enough power through the systems already in place. Some companies have built their own power stations, making excess power available to the local community.

Predicting Problems

Recent technology advances can help prevent accidents and equipment failures, while improving productivity. For example, sensors on machinery can look for early signs of equipment failure. They can monitor the average life-span of equipment so it can be replaced with no break in the work. Sensors can also be used in workers' clothing accessories, such as hats or watches. These can signal when the wearer is in danger. Some even track fatigue, which can cut down on accidents. These technologies are already being used to some extent. They will likely continue to improve and become the standard for large mining operations.

Some mines have invested in renewable energy installations or more energy-efficient equipment. While the primary incentive may be reducing the amount the company spends on energy, the environment also gets some relief because of energy-saving practices. In addition, alternative energy, such as solar or wind power, can be an advantage for mines in remote locations away from existing power grids.

Mines can also adopt the best practices for reducing their water and power usage. Modern technology can help. Businesses can now collect huge amounts of data through devices such as sensors and equipment monitors. Better data monitoring can help reduce energy costs, from the use of fuel to the number of light bulbs. For example, sensors can detect exactly where workers are in a mine. This allows mine operators to turn on lights, climate control, and ventilation only where people are working. Turning off systems in unused areas saves energy. However, the data need to be collected and analyzed properly. Not every mining operation has this technology or uses it to its fullest extent.

WORLDWIDE POLLUTION

Not everyone agrees about how much damage gold mining causes the environment. The US Environmental Protection Agency reported that mining operations have contaminated 40 percent of watershed headways in the western United States. Many of these mines are small, older sites that are no longer in use. Cleaning up these sites may cost more than $35 billion.[3] However, some people claim that strict environmental regulations are working—at least in some states and countries.

Worldwide, gold mining sites are not always subject to such strict rules. Two US companies own gold mines in Indonesia that produce millions of tons of waste each year. One mine is located in the middle of a national park and dumps its waste rock into a river system. The other releases its waste into the ocean. In the latter case, the company has faced criminal charges but denies releasing mining waste into the ocean poses any risk. The company says the mining tailings are harmless, and storing waste in water is safer than storing it on land.

Large gold mining companies typically have policies in place to control their damage to the environment. AngloGold Ashanti has a Social, Ethics and Sustainability Committee to advise the company on safety, health, social, and environmental issues. The company claims several environmental successes. A program involving water resources allowed a native rodent to return to an area where it had been wiped out. The company installed nesting boxes for birds of prey, helping to restore populations that had been previously damaged by ranching practices.

AngloGold Ashanti employees look out over an open-pit mine in Tanzania.

ANGLOGOLD ASHANTI

AngloGold Ashanti is the world's third-largest gold mining company, in terms of production. The company has its headquarters in Johannesburg. It operates seventeen gold mines in nine countries. Most mining operations are in Africa. The company also operates mines and is exploring new possibilities in South America. It has two mining operations in Australia. AngloGold Ashanti produced almost 4 million ounces (113 million g) of gold in 2015. This generated more than $4 billion in income.[4] While the company's primary interest is in gold, it also considers other minerals.

The company employs more than 50,000 people.[5] The company was founded in 1998 through the consolidation of several other South African gold mining companies. It became the first South African company listed on the New York Stock Exchange.

Yet for every success story claimed by a mining company, it seems environmental groups or local citizens are making accusations of bad behavior. AngloGold Ashanti was forced to suspend some mining exploration activities in Colombia in 2013. The local government claimed the mining company had built drilling platforms without permission. A local representative said, "The activities were taking place in a highly fragile agricultural site, and were generating imminent risks and long term damage to the area's land and water."[6]

Other companies show similar discrepancies between their claims and some news reports. Goldcorp states on its website, "Even before one of our mines opens for commercial production, plans are in place for the future reclamation of the land and for the future prosperity of the community after the mine has closed."[7] They cite San Martin, Honduras, as an example of success. The company donated almost six square miles (15.5 sq km) of land to a nonprofit organization.[8] The former mining

Illegal Mining, Extra Pollution

According to the Amazon Conservation Association, more than 30,000 miners are thought to be operating in the Amazon rain forest of Peru without legal permits.[9] They have cut down hundreds of thousands of trees and polluted waterways with the mercury used to process the gold. This has devastated the habitat and endangered human health. In the capital of the area affected, 78 percent of residents have dangerously high levels of mercury in their bodies.[10]

In 2015, the government tasked a special force with destroying 55 illegal mining settlements in the rain forest.[11] Armed police burned homes and shops, leaving the miners and their families homeless. Without better job opportunities, new illegal mining camps are likely to spring up to replace those that are destroyed.

9 | A GOLDEN FUTURE

Gold has come a long way from its roots as a substance used primarily for jewelry and precious objects. Once primarily valued for its pretty color and shine, today, gold's use in electronics shows how important it is to modern life. The metal is also showing up in surprising places. Once again, its special physical properties are of interest. Gold acts as a chemical catalyst. This means it accelerates the rate of chemical reactions without undergoing any changes itself. As such, it can be used in catalytic converters. These devices are used in automobile exhaust systems to convert some pollutants into less harmful compounds.

Gold catalysts are also being developed to reduce water pollution. US university researchers are testing a process to break down hazardous pollutants into nontoxic by-products. The technique uses gold and palladium, another rare metal. It targets chlorinated compounds such as chloroform. Chlorinated compounds were once widely used as solvents, and they have contaminated groundwater around the world. Groundwater will flow through tubes containing thousands of pellets of the palladium and gold catalyst. These create a chemical reaction that breaks down the dangerous chlorinated compounds into two nontoxic substances. Palladium

The gold contacts of a microchip are seen under a microscope.

is the primary catalyst, while gold enhances the reaction. If tests show this process works well, it could help clean up thousands of hazardous waste sites.

Gold can help the environment in other ways as well. Gold nanoparticles, particles of gold at a microscopic scale, can improve how well solar cells work. Solar cells turn the sun's energy into usable power. Their use can reduce the need for using fossil fuels.

Ocean Gold

The world's oceans hold an estimated 20 million short tons (18 metric tons) of gold—enough for each person on Earth to have nine pounds (4 kg) of it.[1] However, most of that gold is in the form of microscopic particles in tiny concentrations found in the seawater. There is currently no practical way to gather and condense that gold. Some larger gold deposits do exist in the rocks on the seafloor. Retrieving this ore can require getting equipment miles deep underwater. Then the gold must be mined from the rock around it and brought to the surface.

IDENTIFYING DISEASE

Gold is also showing up in medicine. The metal rarely has negative effects on the human body. In fact, it resists infection. This is one reason it has been used in dentistry for centuries. The medicinal safety makes it ideal for implantable electronics, a growing field. These small devices can be implanted into a person to monitor his or her vital signs and warn of health dangers. Gold is used in pacemakers, ear implants, and other devices that remain in the body.

Gold nanoparticles also appear in Rapid Diagnostic Tests (RDTs). RDTs are medical tests that can be performed quickly and easily. These tests are especially important in the developing world because they do not require high-tech laboratories. RDTs are frequently used in countries with high rates of malaria. With a single drop of blood, the gold nanoparticles on an RDT change color if certain strains of malaria are present.

Medical scientists are experimenting with other techniques of using gold nanoparticles to detect diseases. For example, gold nanoparticles can help identify proteins related to cancer. In a blood sample, the nanoparticles cluster around the protein, making it easier to spot. Because the nanoparticles help detect the target molecule at very low concentrations, diseases may be identified earlier. Tests for the early detection of prostate cancer and HIV/AIDS are in progress.

Early Medicine

Gold has been used in medicine for thousands of years. In India, gold was one of the metals used in the Ayurvedic system of medicine, which dates back to about 5000 BCE. Finely powdered metals were used both internally and externally. In 2500 BCE, Chinese physicians used gold in treatments for smallpox and skin diseases. Later, the Roman scholar Pliny recommended applying gold to wounds.

SAVING LIVES

Gold cannot only help detect diseases, it can even help prevent or cure some of them. A compound containing gold was used to treat rheumatoid arthritis after World War II. Better forms of treatment have been found, but the medicine is now being explored as a treatment for other illnesses. Studies have shown its effectiveness against giardiasis. This infection, which is caused by a parasite, is very common worldwide. Gold has been shown to destroy the parasite.

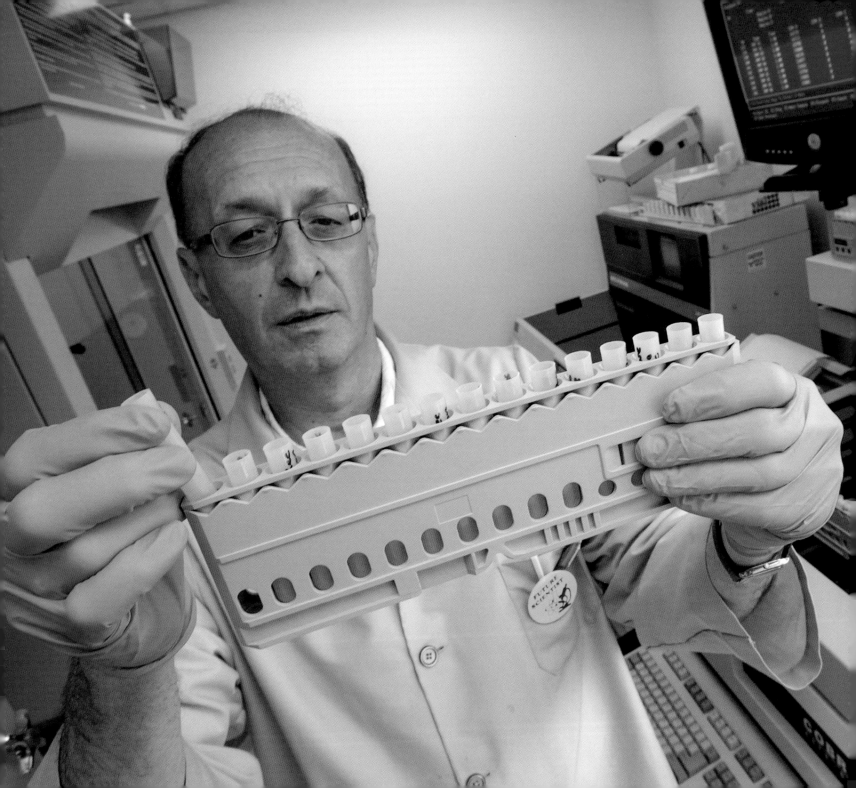

A researcher in Milwaukee, Wisconsin, tests the effects of gold nanoparticles on animal hormones.

Other experiments are testing gold nanoparticles in vaccines. Vaccines help prevent infectious diseases, but many diseases do not yet have a vaccine. Nanoparticles, including gold, may help produce better vaccines against more diseases. Gold nanoparticles are also showing up in experiments to treat cancer. One method undergoing clinical trials uses a drug bound to gold nanoparticles. When injected into the bloodstream, the drug travels to the tumor, targeting it directly. This method causes less damage to the rest of the body than many current cancer treatments. Another treatment undergoing testing injects gold-coated particles of the mineral silica into a tumor. A laser then heats up these particles, destroying the cancer cells with the heat.

A variation of this treatment pairs gold nanoparticles with immune protein antibodies.

The latter latch onto receptors on cancer cells, clustering the particles around the cancer. Short pulses of infrared heat are aimed at the particles to destroy the nearby cancer. The rising heat also vaporizes nearby water molecules. This causes tiny bubbles to expand and burst, ripping apart cancer cells but not healthy tissue. This technique may make it possible to destroy any cancer cells left behind when a tumor is removed. The process is being tested in mice and may go to clinical trials in humans by 2018.

THE FACE OF MINING

Current and upcoming uses for gold mean the demand for gold is likely to stay high. Gold mining operations have a bright future if they can find efficient, safe ways to retrieve gold. The successful operation of a mine depends on mining engineers to supervise the process. Mining engineers are involved at every stage. They may help explore new areas for potential mines; design, build, and operate the mine; and even help restore the land after a mine closes. They may work at the mine site or at corporate headquarters. Jobs typically require at least a bachelor's degree, and the demand for

Finding Metal from Space

Teams of researchers at the US Geological Survey are studying ways to locate mineral resources from space. The system uses instruments aboard a satellite to pinpoint areas likely to contain metal deposits. The goal is to map the world's minerals via satellites. Instruments in the satellite can detect different colors of light on Earth's surface, identifying different materials. The target metal might be found in such small quantities it does not show up on the satellite images. However, geologists can look for other minerals that are often found around the one they want. Initial tests involve mapping known areas with copper deposits. Eventually, the system might be used for identifying many other metal ores, including gold.

workers is expected to grow modestly over the next two decades.

Mining has traditionally been a male occupation. Until the 1970s, many US states had rules prohibiting women from working underground in mines. Today, the mining industry is more accepting of women, and more women are graduating from college mining programs. However, women make up only approximately 13 percent of mining industry employees.[2] Still, many companies are actively recruiting women, and some have set targets for increasing the percentage of women on company boards. Studies have found companies with at least some women on their boards are more profitable than those with all-male boards. Companies with female board members also tend to be rated higher in social and environmental responsibility. "It is an edgy, interesting and challenging industry with a lot of benefits," says Dr. Priscilla Nelson, head of the Department of Mining Engineering at Colorado School of Mines. "The more we can relate that story, the more people will want to get into it, and that includes women."[3]

Women in Mining

Women in Mining is a US educational foundation. It focuses on helping women in the mining industry further their education, as well as helping young people and the general public understand the importance of minerals. Australia has a program called Women in Mining Resources Western Australia. This was established as a networking group for women working in the mining industry. The program includes networking events, an annual seminar, and a mentoring program.

Xoliswa Vanda, the first black woman in South Africa to manage a mining crew, directs workers.

Gender equality is an ongoing goal in the gold industry. A 2016 report revealed a large pay gap among top managers in Australian mining industries. Men were paid on average about $100,000 more per year than women.[4] Still, a degree in mining engineering can lead to good jobs for both men and women. Kathy Steele, chief engineer with Newmont Mining in Phoenix, Arizona, says employees can make anywhere from $65,000 to $150,000. "There is a need for engineers, male or female."[5] She has trouble finding enough qualified mining engineers within the country, so she often has to hire them from abroad.

The world has become dependent on gold for many exciting new uses. Electronics, space exploration, and medicine have expanded the demand for gold beyond jewelry and investments. The gold industry faces challenges as it negotiates ways to mine the precious metal without destroying the land or harming people. New technology will help, along with an industry-wide commitment to the best ethical practices. The gold industry is likely to be an important part of the world's future.

GOLD PRODUCTION 2015

⑤ **CANADA**
331,000 pounds
(150,000 kg)

④ **UNITED STATES**
441,000 pounds
(200,000 kg)

⑧ **MEXICO**
265,000 pounds
(120,000 kg)

⑥ **PERU**
331,000 pounds
(150,000 kg)

RUSSIA
534,000 pounds
(242,000 kg)

CHINA
1,080,000 pounds
(490,000 kg)

UZBEKISTAN
227,000 pounds
(103,000 kg)

GHANA
187,000 pounds
(85,000 kg)

AUSTRALIA
661,000 pounds
(300,000 kg)

SOUTH AFRICA
309,000 pounds
(140,000 kg)

Timeline

3600 BCE
The ancient Egyptians develop a process for smelting gold.

600s BCE
The Etruscans use gold wire to hold animal teeth in place of missing teeth.

500s BCE
The first coins of pure gold with stamped images appear, attributed to King Croesus of Lydia.

1492
Christopher Columbus searches for a western route to Asia and instead finds the Americas, leading the Spanish conquistadors to conquer parts of this new world.

1600s and 1700s
Many well-known scientists practice alchemy, attempting to turn other metals into gold.

1821
The United Kingdom institutes the first gold standard.

1848
James W. Marshall discovers gold near Sutter's Mill in California, setting off the massive 1849 gold rush.

1896
Gold is discovered near Dawson, in the Yukon, setting off the Klondike gold rush.

1890s

The gold recovery process using cyanide is developed.

1930s

After increased prospecting during the Great Depression, the United States shuts down most mining operations during World War II.

1933

The United States goes off the gold standard.

1971

The United States deregulates gold.

1996

The Mars Global Surveyor begins operations in space using a gold-plated telescope mirror.

2004

The environmental group Earthworks launches the No Dirty Gold campaign, asking retail companies not to carry gold produced by mining practices that damage the environment or violate human rights.

2010

The United States passes the Dodd-Frank Wall Street Reform and Consumer Protection Act Section 1502, which requires companies listed in the United States to carry out due diligence on minerals sourced from some African countries.

2030

By this time, the amount of gold that can be retrieved through current methods is expected to drop substantially, if demand continues at the current rate and no major new deposits are found.

Essential Facts

IMPACT ON HISTORY

Gold has been prized for thousands of years and has been used in precious religious and political objects. The quest for gold drove exploration to and through the New World, changing settlement patterns forever. In the process, many native cultures were destroyed. Gold was used directly as money or to back up paper currency until the 1900s and is still an important investment. It is also still used for precious objects such as jewelry, along with new uses in electronics, medicine, and spacecraft parts. The demand for gold is likely to remain high to support these varied uses.

KEY FIGURES

- Christopher Columbus reached the New World while searching for a western route to the spices and gold of Asia. His discovery set off the Spanish conquest of the Americas.

- James W. Marshall found gold at Sutter's Mill in California in 1848, leading thousands of hopeful miners known as '49ers to flood the state.

- The Dodd-Frank Wall Street Reform and Consumer Protection Act provided major financial reforms. It required companies listed in the United States to carry out due diligence on minerals sourced from some African countries. The act was named after US Representative Barney Frank and Senator Chris Dodd, who were active in introducing it.

- The World Gold Council, an industry group, establishes policy for large gold mining operations, including the Conflict-Free Gold Standard to prevent human rights abuses.

- The US Bureau of Land Management offers advice and maps to help amateur or professional prospectors find suitable areas for prospecting.

KEY STATISTICS

▶ Approximately 100,000 people headed to the Yukon during the Klondike gold rush, but only 30,000 people were able to complete the strenuous trip.

▶ Pure gold is called 24 karat gold, while 14 karat gold—composed of 14 parts of gold and 10 parts of other metals—is often used in jewelry.

▶ The gold bars in Fort Knox each weigh around 400 troy ounces, or 27.5 pounds (12.5 kg).

▶ Women make up only approximately 13 percent of mining industry employees, but the number of women in mining is increasing.

▶ By 2030, the gold supply may be running out unless major new deposits are found or new gold retrieval methods are developed.

▶ The world's oceans hold an estimated 22 million tons (20 million metric tons) of gold, but there is currently no practical way to collect it.

QUOTE

"It is important that international and domestic business, governments, civil society and consumers all play their part in raising standards and encouraging responsible global trade."

– The World Gold Council

...ning two or more metals or a
...l.

amalgam

A mixture or blend of mercury and other metals.

catalyst

A substance that increases the rate of chemical reactions without undergoing any changes itself.

conquistador

A conqueror, especially one of the Spanish or Portuguese soldiers who defeated the native civilizations of Latin America in the 1500s.

corrosion

The breaking down of a material, especially a metal, through chemical reactions.

currency

A system of money used in a particular country.

industrial mineral

Geologic material that is mined for its commercial value, not including metals or fuel.

karat

A standard to describe the purity of gold, with pure gold being 24 karat.

lode

A vein of metal that fills a crack or space in rock.

mining claim

A miner's legal right to explore and extract minerals from a specific piece of land.

nanoparticle

A particle at a microscopic scale.

open-pit mining

A mining process in which a large pit is dug on the surface of the earth.

ore

Mineral or rock from which a useful or valuable substance, such as a metal, can be extracted.

placer

Sand or gravel deposited by rivers, containing heavy minerals such as gold.

shareholder

An individual or group that owns shares in a company.

sluice box

An artificial channel for moving water.

slurry

A semiliquid mixture of rock and water that results from some mining processes.

smelting

A process of heating and melting to separate gold from the surrounding ore.

tarnish

To lose brightness, especially by exposure to air.

Additional Resources

SELECTED BIBLIOGRAPHY

Kirkemo, Harold, William L. Newman, and Roger P. Ashley. "Gold: A Brief History of Prospecting, Mining and Production." *Geology.com*. Geology.com, 2016. Web. 21 June 2016.

"Tracking the Trends 2016." *Deloitte*. Deloitte, 2016. Web. 21 June 2016.

"What Do Mining Engineers Do?" *UNSW Australia*. UNSW Engineering, n.d. Web. 21 June 2016.

FURTHER READINGS

Grayson, Robert. *California's Gold Rush*. Minneapolis: Abdo, 2012.

Lusted, Marcia Amidon. *The Chilean Miners' Rescue*. Minneapolis: Abdo, 2012.

Sheinkin, Steve. *Which Way to the Wild West?: Everything Your Schoolbooks Didn't Tell You about America's Westward Expansion*. New York: Roaring Brook, 2009.

WEBSITES

To learn more about Big Business, visit **booklinks.abdopublishing.com**. These links are routinely monitored and updated to provide the most current information available.

FOR MORE INFORMATION

For more information on this subject, contact or visit the following organizations:

Alabama Gold Camp

1398 County Road 5
Lineville, AL 36266
256-396-0389
http://alabamagoldcamp.com

Families can camp and stay at the Alabama Gold Camp. Activities include sluicing, panning, and dredging in the river.

Columbia State Historic Park

11255 Jackson Street
Columbia, CA 95310
209-588-9128
http://www.parks.ca.gov/?page_id=552

Step back into a 1850s gold mining town with costumed tour guides and hands-on crafts and activities, including gold panning.

Marshall Gold Discovery

310 Back Street
Coloma, CA 95613
530-622-3470
http://www.parks.ca.gov/?page_id=484

Visit the small town of Coloma, California, and see where James Marshall first discovered gold in the American River leading to the 1849 gold rush.

Source Notes

CHAPTER 1. GOLD IN SPACE

1. "NASA's Webb Telescope Completes Mirror-Coating Milestone." *NASA*. NASA, 13 Sept. 2011. Web. 29 June 2016.

2. "Modern Uses of Gold." *Gold Resource*. GoldResource.net, 31 Jan. 2013. Web. 29 June 2016.

3. Ibid.

4. "Which Metals Conduct Electricity?" *Metal Supermarkets*. Metal Supermarkets, 22 Sept. 2015. Web. 29 June 2016.

CHAPTER 2. THE AGE OF EXPLORATION

1. Joshua J. Mark. "Croesus." *Ancient History Encyclopedia*. Ancient History Encyclopedia, 2 Sept. 2009. Web. 29 June 2016.

2. Mike Leahy. "Gold Smelting." *PBS*. Open University, 2005. Web. 29 June 2016.

3. "The Vision." *PBS*. West Film Project, 2001. Web. 29 June 2016.

4. Michael Wood. "The Story of the Conquistadors." *BBC*. BBC, 29 Mar. 2011. Web. 29 June 2016.

5. Ibid.

CHAPTER 3. THE RUSH FOR RICHES

1. "World Gold Deposits." *American Museum of Natural History*. American Museum of Natural History, n.d. Web. 29 June 2016.

2. Harold Kirkemo, William L. Newman, and Roger P. Ashley. "Gold." *Geology.com*. Geology.com, 2016. Web. 29 June 2016.

3. "Troy Ounce vs. Ounce." *Gold Price*. Gold Price, 27 Dec. 2012. Web. 29 June 2016.

4. "The Gold Rush of 1849." *History.com*. A&E Networks, 2010. Web. 29 June 2016.

5. Ibid.

6. Ibid.

7. "Gold Rush." *Encyclopædia Britannica*. Encyclopædia Britannica, 2016. Web. 29 June 2016.

8. Alysa Landry. "Native History: California Gold Rush Begins, Devastates Native Population." *Indian Country Today Media Network*. Indian Country Today Media Network, 24 Jan. 2014. Web. 29 June 2016.

9. "Fort Collins History and Architecture." *Fort Collins History Connection*. City of Fort Collins, 2012. Web. 29 June 2016.

10. "The Klondike Gold Rush." *University of Washington*. University of Washington Libraries, n.d. Web. 29 June 2016.

CHAPTER 4. NEW MINING METHODS

1. "Mining History and Geology of the California Gold Rush." *Modesto Junior College*. Modesto Junior College, n.d. Web. 29 June 2016.

2. Devon Coquillard. "If It Can't Be Grown, It Has to Be Mined (and Manufactured)." *TheMoreYouDig*. TheMoreYouDig, 2 Feb. 2016. Web. 29 June 2016.

3. Charles N. Alpers, Michael P. Hunerlach, Jason T. May, and Roger L. Hothem. "Mercury Contamination from Historical Gold Mining in California." *USGS*. US Department of Interior, 17 Feb. 2016. Web. 29 June 2016.

4. "Mining History and Geology of the California Gold Rush." *Modesto Junior College*. Modesto Junior College, n.d. Web. 29 June 2016.

5. Harold Kirkemo, William L. Newman, and Roger P. Ashley. "Gold." *Geology.com*. Geology.com, 2016. Web. 29 June 2016.

6. "Mining History and Geology of the California Gold Rush." *Modesto Junior College*. Modesto Junior College, n.d. Web. 29 June 2016.

7. Harold Kirkemo, William L. Newman, and Roger P. Ashley. "Gold." *Geology.com*. Geology.com, 2016. Web. 29 June 2016.

8. Hobart King. "The Many Uses of Gold." *Geology.com*. Geology.com, 2016. Web. 29 June 2016.

9. Harold Kirkemo, William L. Newman, and Roger P. Ashley. "Gold." *Geology.com*. Geology.com, 2016. Web. 29 June 2016.

10. Mark Cartwright. "Gold in Antiquity." *Ancient History Encyclopedia*. Ancient History Encyclopedia, 4 Apr. 2014. Web. 29 June 2016.

CHAPTER 5. BECOMING BIG BUSINESS

1. "Frequently Asked Questions about Sulfide Mining in Minnesota: A Mining Truth Report." *Conservation Minnesota*. MiningTruth.org, May 2012. Web. 29 June 2016.

2. Vladimir Basov. "Heap Leach: Mining's Breakthrough Technology." *Mining.com*. Mining.com, 20 Aug. 2015. Web. 29 June 2016.

3. Justin Rowlatt. "Why Do We Value Gold?" *BBC*. BBC, 8 Dec. 2013. Web. 29 June 2016.

4. "Modern Uses of Gold." *Gold Resource*. GoldResource.net, 31 Jan. 2013. Web. 29 June 2016.

5. Devon Coquillard. "If It Can't Be Grown, It Has to Be Mined (and Manufactured)." *TheMoreYouDig*. TheMoreYouDig, 2 Feb. 2016. Web. 29 June 2016.

Source Notes Continued

CHAPTER 6. ECONOMIC EFFECTS

1. Suzanne Daley. "Guatemalan Women's Claims Put Focus on Canadian Firms' Conduct Abroad." *New York Times*. New York Times Company, 2 Apr. 2016. Web. 29 June 2016.

2. "About Barrick Gold Corporation." *Barrick*. Barrick Gold Corporation, 2016. Web. 29 June 2016.

3. Amrutha Gayathri. "Barrick to Spend about $2 Billion on Nevada, Peru Projects." *Business News Network*. Bell Media, 22 Feb. 2016. Web. 29 June 2016.

4. "Why Barrick?" *Barrick*. Barrick Gold Corporation, 2016. Web. 29 June 2016.

5. Sue George. "Gold Mining and Conflict: How Effective Are Regulations?" *Guardian*. Guardian News and Media, 2 May 2013. Web. 29 June 2016.

6. Donovan Webster. "The Devastating Costs of the Amazon Gold Rush." *Smithsonian.com*. Smithsonian.com, Feb. 2012. Web. 29 June 2016.

7. Ibid.

8. Ibid.

9. "Responsible Gold Sourcing." *World Gold Council*. World Gold Council, 2016. Web. 29 June 2016.

10. "Tracking the Trends 2016." *Deloitte*. Deloitte, 2016. Web. 29 June 2016.

11. Ibid.

12. Ibid.

13. "Aboriginal & Indigenous People." *Goldcorp*. Goldcorp, n.d. Web. 29 June 2016.

14. "An Interview with Peter Munk." *Economist*. Economist Newspaper, 29 Apr. 2014. Web. 29 June 2016.

15. Sue George. "Gold Mining and Conflict: How Effective Are Regulations?" *Guardian*. Guardian News and Media, 2 May 2013. Web. 29 June 2016.

16. "Responsible Gold Sourcing." *World Gold Council*. World Gold Council, 2016. Web. 29 June 2016.

17. Ibid.

CHAPTER 7. PROTECTING PEOPLE

1. "Responsible Gold Sourcing." *World Gold Council*. World Gold Council, 2016. Web. 29 June 2016.

2. Sue George. "Gold Mining and Conflict: How Effective Are Regulations?" *Guardian*. Guardian News and Media, 2 May 2013. Web. 29 June 2016.

3. David Hill. "Welcome to Guatemala: Gold Mine Protester Beaten and Burnt Alive." *Guardian*. Guardian News and Media, 12 Aug. 2014. Web. 29 June 2016.

4. May-Ying Lam. "Inside a Gold Mining Crackdown Operation in the Amazon." *Washington Post*. Washington Post, 28 Apr. 2016. Web. 29 June 2016.

5. Kevin Crowley. "NYU Graduates Seeking $11 Billion of Gold in Ransacked Mine." *Bloomberg*. Bloomberg, 5 Apr. 2016. Web. 29 June 2016.

6. Ibid.

7. Kevin Sieff. "South Africa's Gold Industry, Like Its Economy, Is Crumbling." *Washington Post*. Washington Post, 7 Mar. 2016. Web. 29 June 2016.

8. Kevin Crowley. "NYU Graduates Seeking $11 Billion of Gold in Ransacked Mine." *Bloomberg*. Bloomberg, 5 Apr. 2016. Web. 29 June 2016.

CHAPTER 8. DIGGING THE LAND

1. Alastair Bland. "The Environmental Disaster That Is the Gold Industry." *Smithsonian.com*. Smithsonian.com, 14 Feb. 2014. Web. 29 June 2016.

2. "Tracking the Trends 2016." *Deloitte*. Deloitte, 2016. Web. 29 June 2016.

3. Alastair Bland. "The Environmental Disaster That Is the Gold Industry." *Smithsonian.com*. Smithsonian.com, 14 Feb. 2014. Web. 29 June 2016.

4. "A Truly Global Producer of Gold." *AngloGold Ashanti*. AngloGold Ashanti, 2014. Web. 29 June 2016.

5. "Supporting Our Strategy." *AngloGold Ashanti*. AngloGold Ashanti, 2014. Web. 29 June 2016.

6. "AngloGold Ashanti Operations Suspended in Colombia." *Ethical Consumer*. Ethical Consumer Research, 22 Mar. 2013. Web. 29 June 2016.

7. "Mine Closure & Reclamation." *Goldcorp*. Goldcorp, n.d. Web. 29 June 2016.

8. Ibid.

9. "Fact Sheet: Illegal Gold Mining in Madre de Dios, Peru." *Amazon Conservation Association*. AmazonConservation.org, n.d. Web. 29 June 2016.

10. Ibid.

11. Imogen Calderwood. "The End of the Gold Rush." *Daily Mail*. Daily Mail, 25 July 2015. Web. 29 June 2016.

12. Alastair Bland. "The Environmental Disaster That Is the Gold Industry." *Smithsonian.com*. Smithsonian.com, 14 Feb. 2014. Web. 29 June 2016.

13. Ibid.

CHAPTER 9. A GOLDEN FUTURE

1. "Is There Gold in the Ocean?" *National Ocean Service*. NOAA, 24 June 2014. Web. 29 June 2016.

2. Lisa Marshall. "Are Women the Mining Industry's Most Underdeveloped Resource?" *Mines*. Mines Magazine, 25 Apr. 2014. Web. 29 June 2016.

3. Ibid.

4. "Gender Pay Gap in Mining Sector." *WIMWA*. WIMWA, 3 Mar. 2016. Web. 29 June 2016.

5. Lisa Marshall. "Are Women the Mining Industry's Most Underdeveloped Resource?" *Mines*. Mines Magazine, 25 Apr. 2014. Web. 29 June 2016.

Index

ABOUT THE AUTHOR

M. M. Eboch writes about science, history, and culture for all ages. Her recent nonfiction titles include *Chaco Canyon*, *Living with Dyslexia*, and *The Green Movement*. Her novels for young people include *The Genie's Gift*, a Middle Eastern fantasy; *The Eyes of Pharaoh*, a mystery in ancient Egypt; *The Well of Sacrifice*, a Mayan adventure; and the Haunted series, which starts with *The Ghost on the Stairs*.

BOOK CHARGING CARD

Accession No.＿＿＿＿＿＿＿＿＿＿ Call No.＿＿＿＿＿＿

Author＿＿＿＿＿＿＿＿＿＿＿＿＿＿＿＿＿＿＿＿＿＿

Title＿＿＿＿＿＿＿＿＿＿＿＿＿＿＿＿＿＿＿＿＿＿＿

Date Loaned	Borrower's Name	Date Ret...